This journal belongs to

_____

_____

GRIEF
GUIDE

creating a
pathway to
resilience
and recovery

Thank you for choosing this interactive, holistic, creative self-help journal.

Its purpose is to promote and enable a unique understanding of the fluid stages of grief.

With your investment of time, this guide will transform into a privatised living memoir of your grief journey.

Within these pages you will explore the theories, moods, thoughts, feelings and emotions surrounding your grief episode. By journaling, drawing and scribbling, this resource can aid and reduce stress, offer clarity and enhance well-being, while encouraging you to recognise your behaviours and responses.

CONTEN[TS]

p01 FOREWORD

p03 Stage 1 INTRODUCTION TO GRIEF

In this opening chapter, you can learn how to understand loss through Kubler-Ross's Five Stages of Grief. You will also explore how well-being is affected over time from the initial stages of denial right through to the recovery stage.

p19 Stage 2 EMOTIONS AND FEELINGS

This chapter offers a deeper exploration into how grief can affect you and to recognise when it appears as feelings, physical sensations and behaviours. Then, by investigating the trauma cycle, you may be able to 'write a letter to grief', which can help you recognise, categorise and understand that this is very 'normal' in the stages of loss.

Colour coded stages

The FLUID STAGES OF GRIEF are colour coded from dark to light and mirror your journey from sadness towards relief and healing.

ADVANCEMENT Stage 3

p53

By introducing deconstruction and reconstruction, you'll examine the constantly changing qualities of life and the waves of guilt, blame and despair. Through the support of friends and family networks and other coping strategies, you can recognise how those connections begin to foster real change.

REVELATION Stage 4

p75

Working with newly developed skills, you may be able to answer questions with greater compassion toward your suffering. In this calmer space, you are encouraged to nurture that strength and gather photographs, letters and notes and reflect on memories. Use this stage to review your time-line of grief, and then to process and reflect.

USEFUL CONTACTS p86

ABOUT THE AUTHOR p89

FOREWORD

As a qualified psychotherapist working within the field of bereavement for many years, I have designed this journal for teens and young adults to help process the experience of grief and loss.
It was created with *YOU* in mind!

PAUSE FOR THOUGHT

Move through this book at your own pace - pause for thought and allow yourself to process and reflect on each realisation as and when it appears. There are no right or wrong emotions or answers. As you explore, feel free to use hieroglyphs, notes scripts, drawings, photographs, or simply scribble your responses.

Using a combination of images, poems and texts, each chapter walks with you through the various 'normal' stages on the time-line of grief. When I felt it necessary to focus on a particular area, I have clarified by introducing both clinical and non-clinical vocabulary.

The journey I took to create this journal became part of my own healing process - helping me to overcome recent losses. I trust my commitment and energy connect with your journey and when you come to a place of understanding, you may develop patience and compassion leading to a healing of your own.

K. B. Whelan

K.B.WHELAN MA. BA (HONS) DFAP. MBACP/ACCRE MNCS PG DIP.

PS: My guidance on grief is that you allow for 3-9 months, or if you feel immediate support is needed, you are the best judge. During this time (especially if you are under 18) you can talk with your family, parents or guardians. This allows your body, mind and spirit to process your loss naturally. Meanwhile, you may find a private space for your thoughts here - remember you only need to share this journal with others if you feel it is right for you ...

Introduction to Grief

STAGE 1

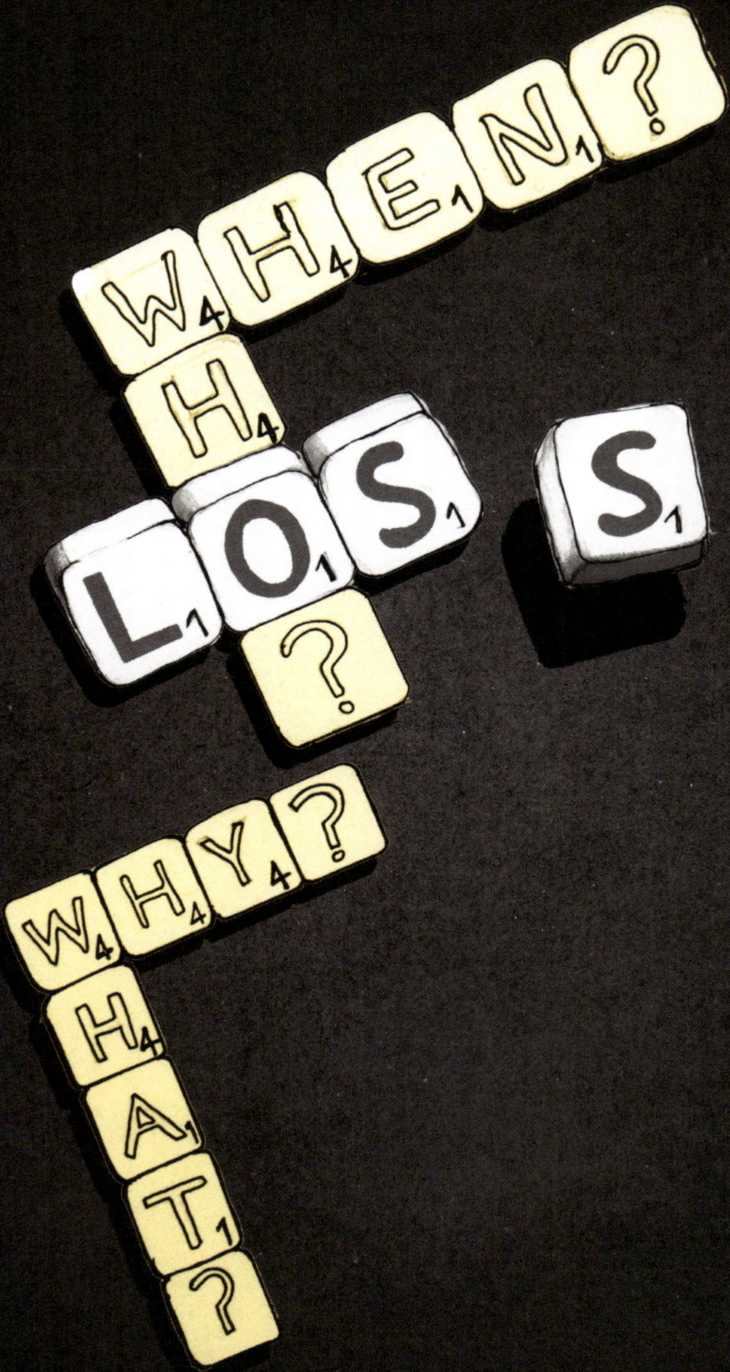
WHEN?
WHO?
LOSS
WHY?
WHAT?

GRIEF CAN LEAVE YOU FEELING...

Caught up

Ambivalent

Holding emotions and feelings

Hyper sensitive

Insular

Tense

Remote

Edgy

BALL OF GRIEF

Emotive

Angry

Wound up

Discombobulated

Volatile

Mistrusting of others and yourself

Avoiding Connections

ALL NORMAL ALL NORMAL ALL NORMAL

PAUSE FOR THOUGHT

FIVE STAGES OF GRIEF

KÜBLER-ROSS

 **Dr. Elisabeth Kübler-Ross** pioneered methods used in the support and counselling of those experiencing personal trauma, death and dying. She also dramatically improved the understanding and practices in relation to bereavement and hospice care.

Her ideas, notably the five stages of grief model (denial, anger, bargaining, depression, acceptance), are also transferable to personal change and emotional upset resulting from factors other than death and dying.

1. Denial

Denial is a conscious or unconscious refusal to accept facts, information, reality, etc., relating to the situation concerned. It's a defence mechanism and perfectly natural. Some people can become locked in this stage when dealing with a traumatic change that can be ignored. Death of course is not particularly easy to avoid or evade indefinitely.

2. Anger

Anger can manifest in different ways. People dealing with emotional upset can be angry with themselves, and/or with others, especially those close to them. Knowing this helps one to keep detached and non-judgemental when experiencing the anger of someone who is very upset.

3. Bargaining

Traditionally the bargaining stage for people facing death can involve attempting to bargain with whatever God the person believes in. People facing less serious trauma can bargain or seek to negotiate a compromise.

For example "Can we still be friends?" when facing a break-up. Bargaining rarely provides a sustainable solution, especially if it's a matter of life or death.

4. Depression

Also referred to as preparatory grieving. In a way it's the dress rehearsal or the practice run for the 'aftermath' although this stage means different things depending on whom it involves. It's a sort of acceptance with emotional attachment. It's natural to feel sadness and regret, fear, uncertainty, etc. It shows that the person has at least begun to accept the reality.

5. Acceptance

Again this stage definitely varies according to the person's situation, although broadly it is an indication that there is some emotional detachment and objectivity. People dying can enter this stage a long time before the people they leave behind, who must necessarily pass through their own stages of dealing with the grief.

PAUSE FOR THOUGHT

PROCESS

Initial Stage
* Disbelief
* Busyness
* Denial
* _____
* _____
* _____

Falling Stage
* Development of 'negative' feelings
* Anger *Guilt
* Frustration
* Helplessness
* _____
* _____
* _____

TIME LINE

ING LOSS

Depressive Stage
* Hopelessness
* Lethargy
* Loneliness
* Inability to cope
* _____
* _____
* _____

Recovery Stage
* Putting loss into context
* Reconnecting
* Rebuilding life
* Looking forward to chances in life without the person, thing or close relationship
* _____
* _____
* _____

PAUSE FOR THOUGHT

Write

Reflect

EMOTIONS & FEELINGS

STAGE 2

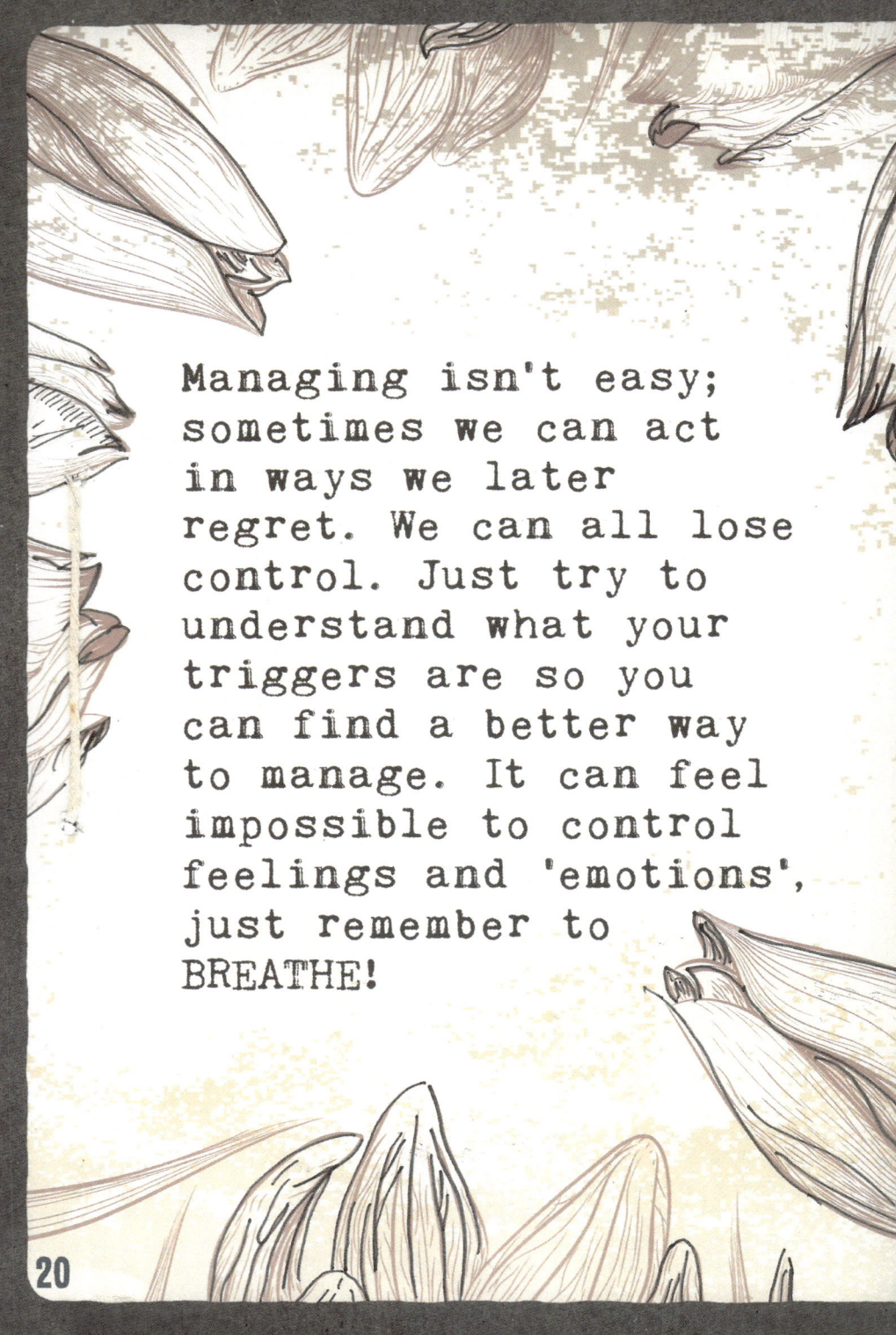

Managing isn't easy; sometimes we can act in ways we later regret. We can all lose control. Just try to understand what your triggers are so you can find a better way to manage. It can feel impossible to control feelings and 'emotions', just remember to BREATHE!

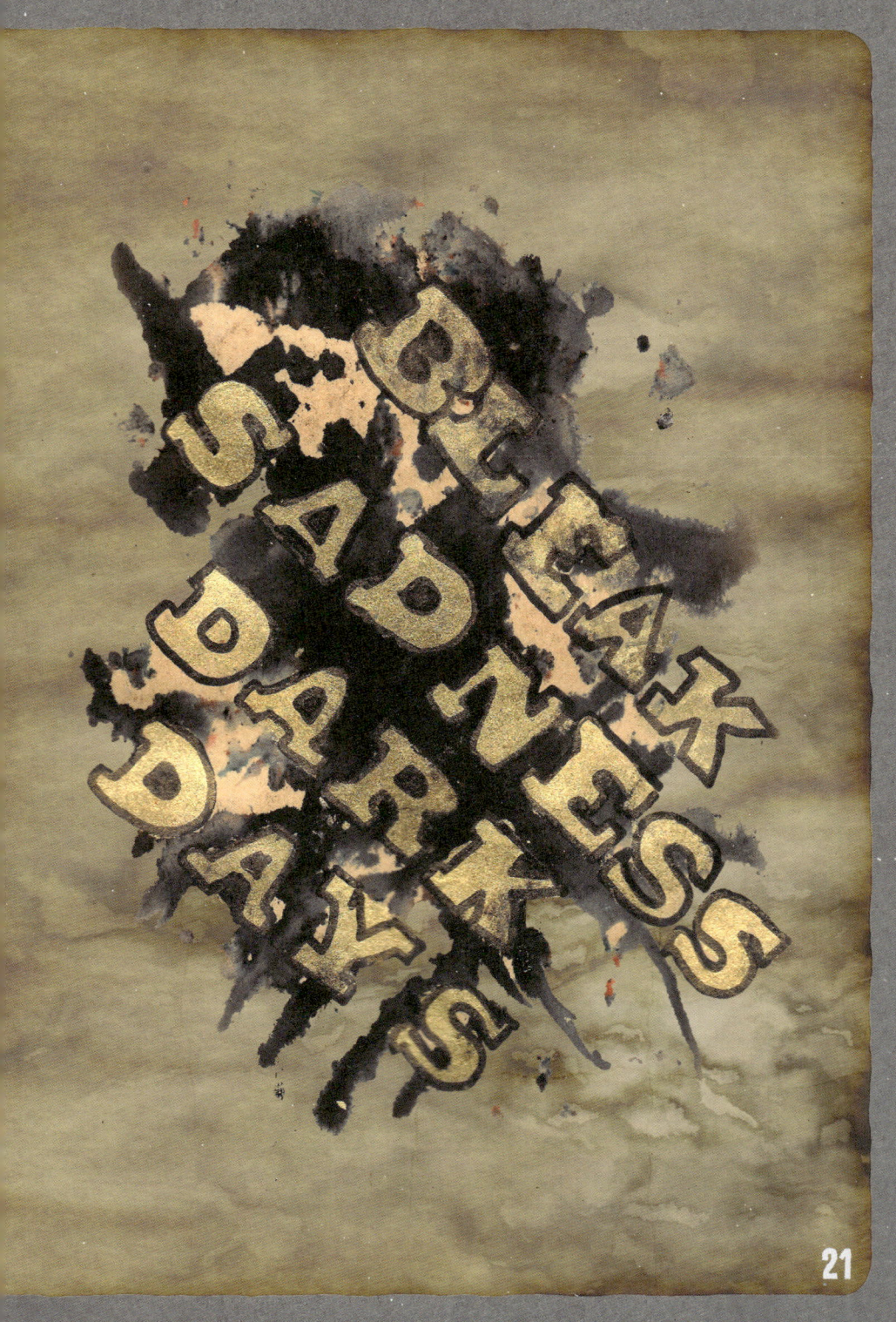

PAUSE FOR THOUGHT

Write

Reflect

DRAW

RECOGNISE Y

_____

_____

_____

24

OUR FEELINGS

_____

_____

_____

25

RECOGNISE Y

_____

_____

_____

UR EMOTIONS

_____

_____

_____

IDENTIFY YO

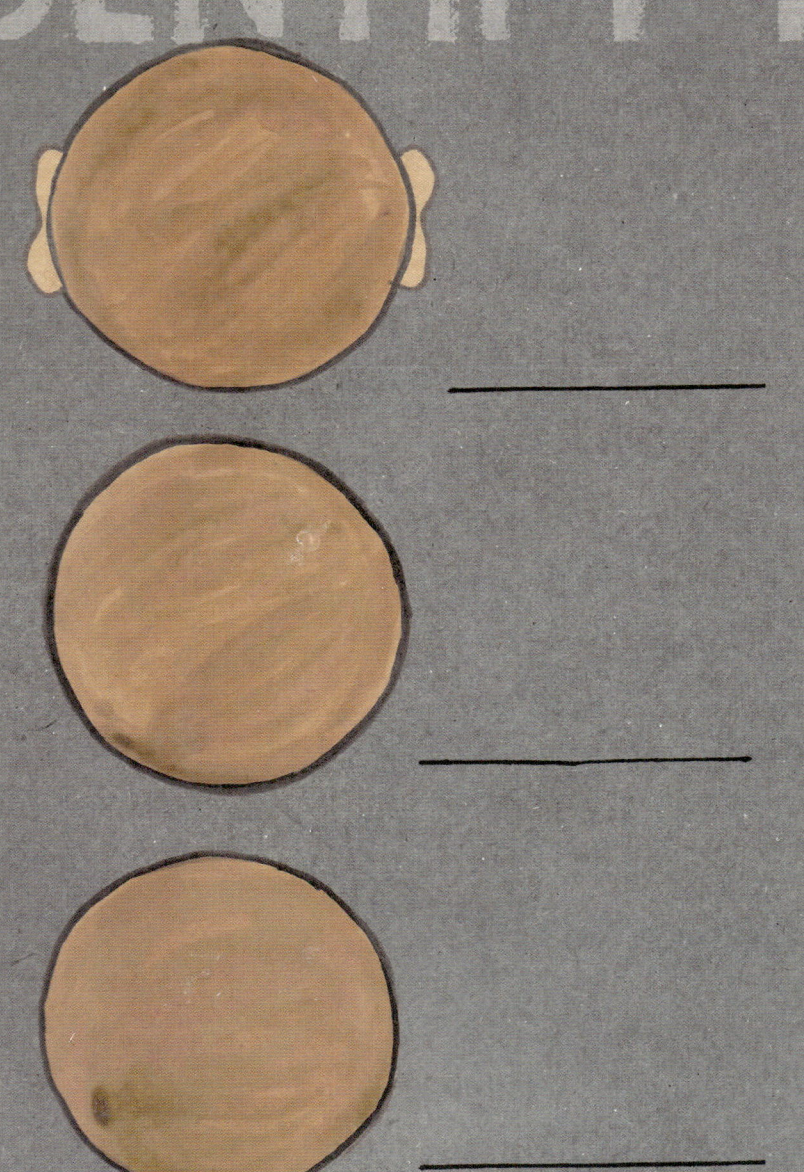

UR FEELINGS

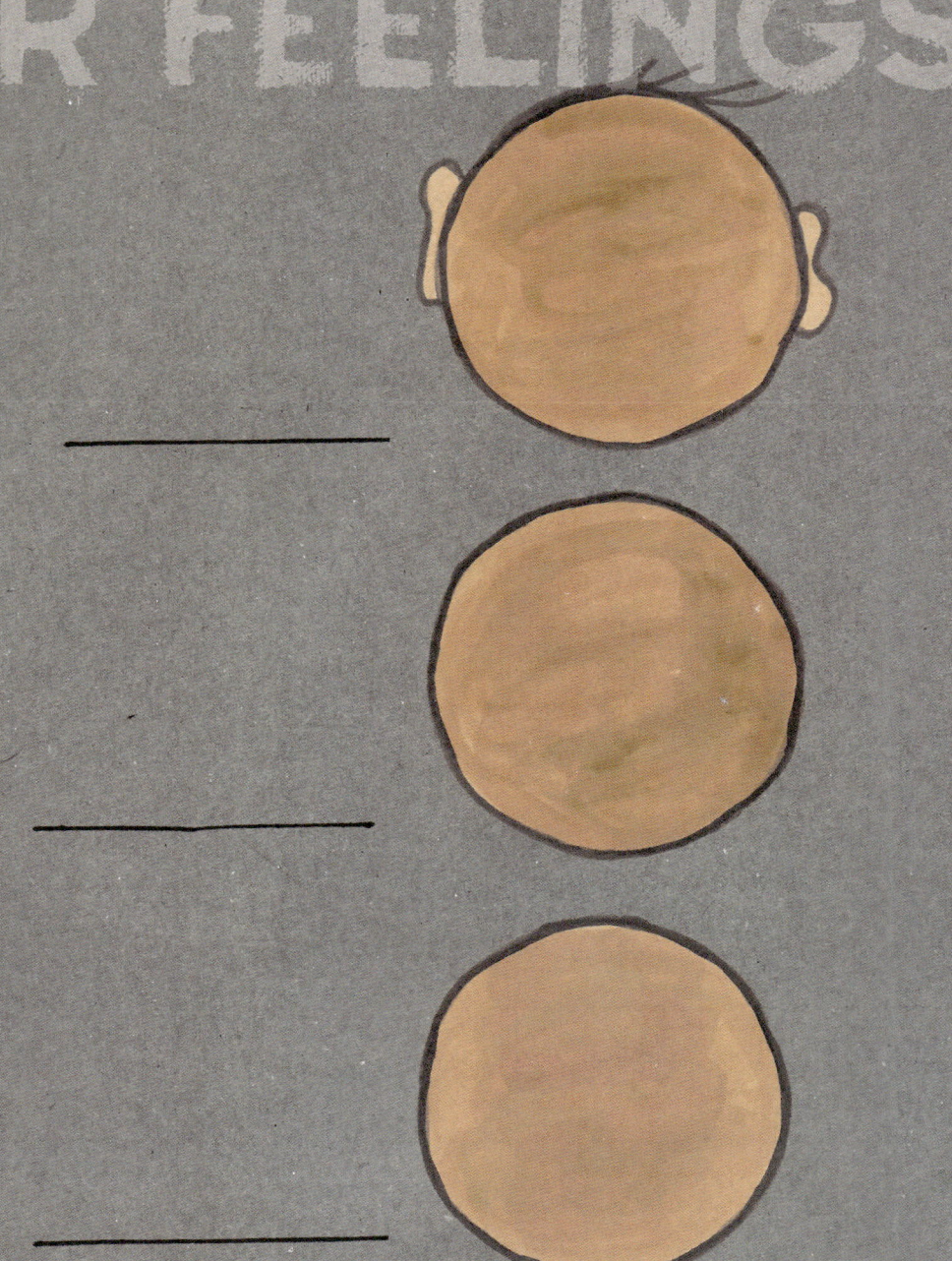

_____

_____

_____

29

Sometimes it can feel like you are

31

Nightmares
Flashbacks

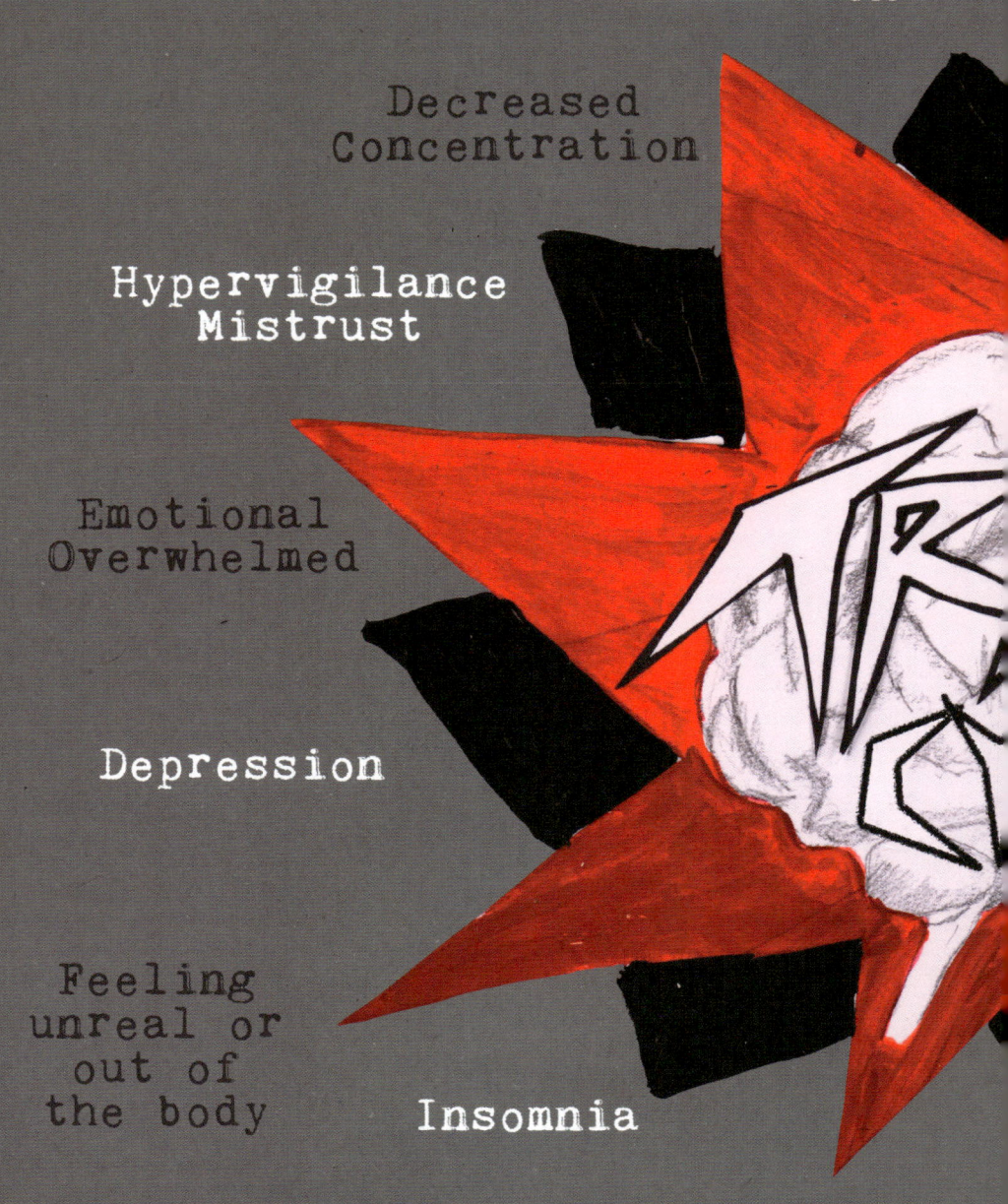

Decreased
Concentration

Hypervigilance
Mistrust

Emotional
Overwhelmed

Depression

Feeling
unreal or
out of
the body

Insomnia

Chronic pain
Headaches

Loss of
a sense of
'Who I am'

Numbing

Irritability

General
anxiety
or panic
attacks

Little
or no
memories

Loss of
interest

Loss of
a sense
of the
future

Self-destructive
behaviour

IT CAN GET CONFUSING...

words.

Exhausted · Mismanagement · confused · survival · hurt · dead · frustrated · abandoned · sad · died · angry · worn · weak

PAUSE FOR THOUGHT

analyse

DRAW

This wheel shows the stages of grief emotion...

ANGRY
- Jealous
- Selfish
- Ashamed
- Mean
- Demanding
- Judgemental
- Hurt
- Frustrated
- Hateful
- Critical
- Bitter
- Irritated

SCARED
- Embarrassed
- Unmotivated
- Unenthusiastic
- Indifferent
- Resilient
- Grotty
- Confused
- Helpless
- Compliant
- Foolish
- Weak
- Preoccupied

HAPPY
- Communication
- Carefree
- Constructive
- Adventurous
- Heartful
- Kind
- Excited
- Loving
- Energetic
- Optimistic
- Creative
- Content

...but there is space here for you to add your own

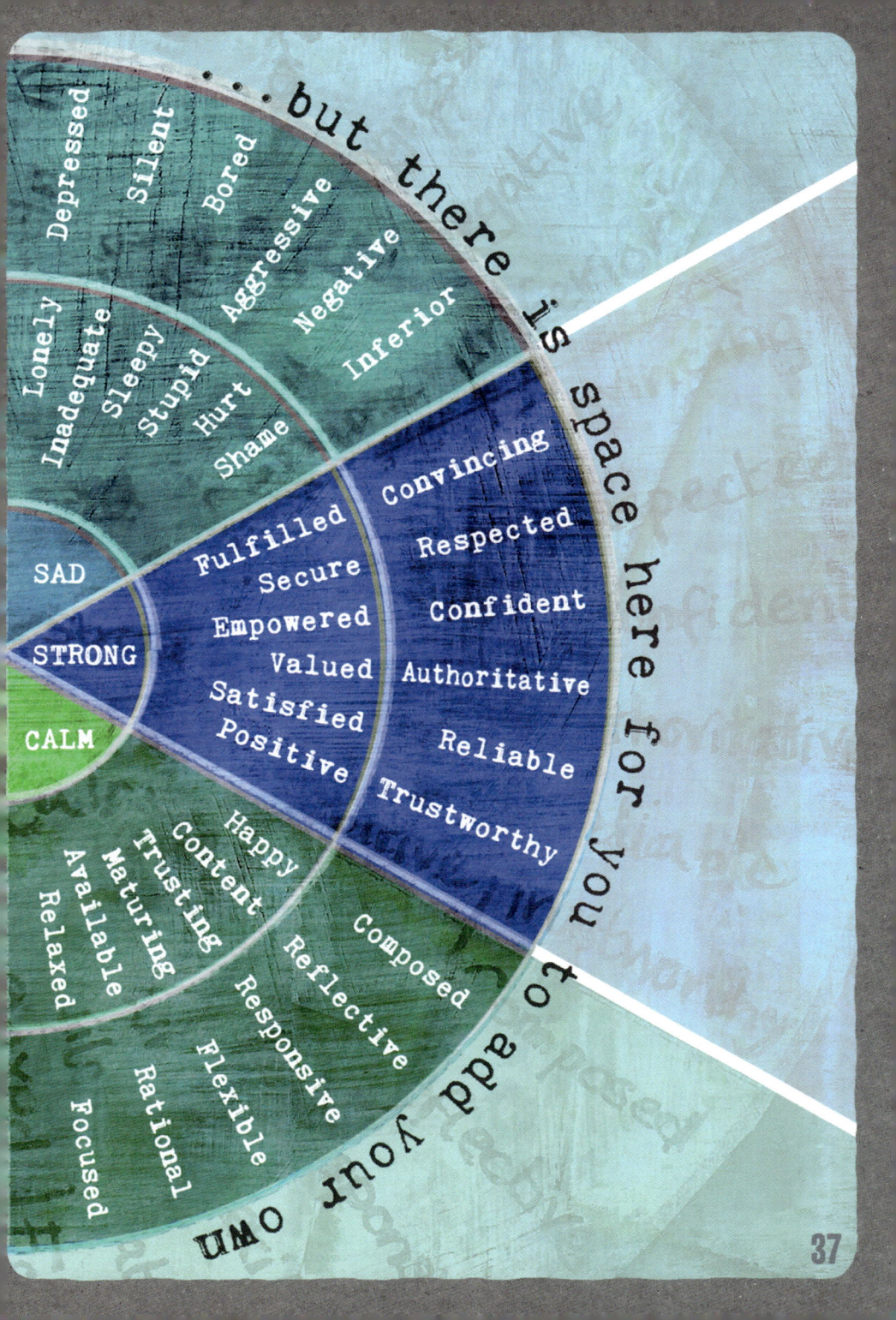

SAD
- Depressed
- Silent
- Bored
- Aggressive
- Negative
- Inferior
- Lonely
- Inadequate
- Sleepy
- Stupid
- Hurt
- Shame

STRONG
- Fulfilled
- Secure
- Empowered
- Valued
- Satisfied
- Positive
- Convincing
- Respected
- Confident
- Authoritative
- Reliable
- Trustworthy

CALM
- Happy
- Content
- Trusting
- Maturing
- Available
- Relaxed
- Composed
- Reflective
- Responsive
- Flexible
- Rational
- Focused

37

IF FEELINGS COULD TALK

SADNESS might be telling me to CRY

LONELINESS might be telling me I need SELF COMPASSION

RESENTMENT might be telling me I need to FORGIVE

EMPTINESS might be telling me I need to do something CREATIVE

ANGER might be telling me I need to check-in with my BOUNDARIES

ANXIETY might be telling me to be BRAVE

STRESS might be telling me I need to take ONE STEP AT A TIME

FEAR might be telling me to survive this JOURNEY

PAUSE FOR THOUGHT

FEELINGS

Emotions

MANIFESTAIONS

Numbness Anger Isolation

Anxiety

SHOCK!

Relief **FEELINGS**
CIRCLE THE WORDS THAT APPLY TO YOU
AND ADD YOUR OWN

Sadness Reproach

Guilt and
self reproach

Loneliness Fatigue

Pining and Helplessness
yearning

Freedom

OF 'NORMAL' GRIEF

Dry Mouth

Hollowness in the Stomach

Anxious

PHYSICAL SENSATION
CIRCLE THE WORDS THAT APPLY TO YOU AND ADD YOUR OWN

Tightness in the throat and chest

Sensitive to noise

Lack of energy

Restless

MANIFESTAIONS OF 'NORMAL' GRIEF

BEHAVIOURS
CIRCLE THE WORDS THAT APPLY TO YOU AND ADD YOUR OWN

- Sleep disturbance
- Visits to special places
- Dreams of deceased
- Reflecting
- Emotional
- SHOUTING!!!
- Sighing
- Overactive
- Crying (hysterically)
- Treating objects and belongings with preciousness
- Searching...
- Talking to deceased
- Outbursts
- SCREAMING!
- Appetite Disturbance
- Hysterical
- Oversensitive
- Isolation

NORMALNESS
LEADS
TO SADNESS
-PHIL LESTER

PAUSE FOR THOUGHT

Reflect

WRITE

DRAW

STROBE A[ND]
DUAL MO[DEL]
EVERYDAY LIFE

LOSS-ORIENTATED

GRIEF WORK
INTRUSION OF GRIEF
BREAKING BONDS AND TIES
RELOCATION
DENIAL
AVOIDANCE OF RESTORATION CHANGES

CONCEPT OF OSCILLATION 'NORMAL BEHAVIOUR'

ND SCHUT
L OF GRIEF

EXPERIENCE

RESTORATION-ORIENTATED

ATTENDING TO LIFE CHANGES

DOING NEW THINGS

DISTRACTIONS FROM GRIEF

DENIAL AND AVOIDANCE OF GRIEF

NEW ROLES AND IDENTITIES RELATIONSHIPS

RECOVERY AND NORMALITY WITH A DIFFERENCE

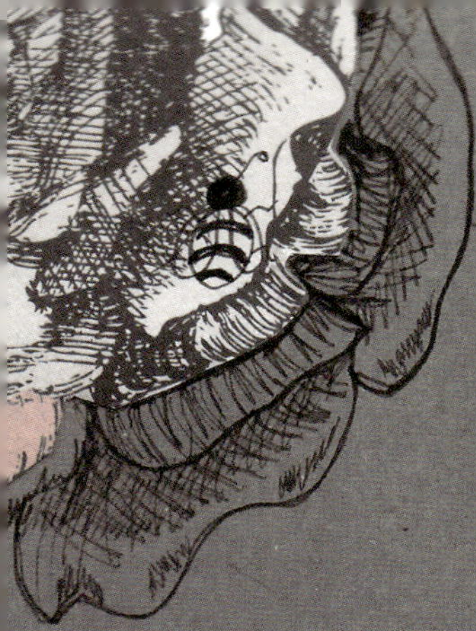

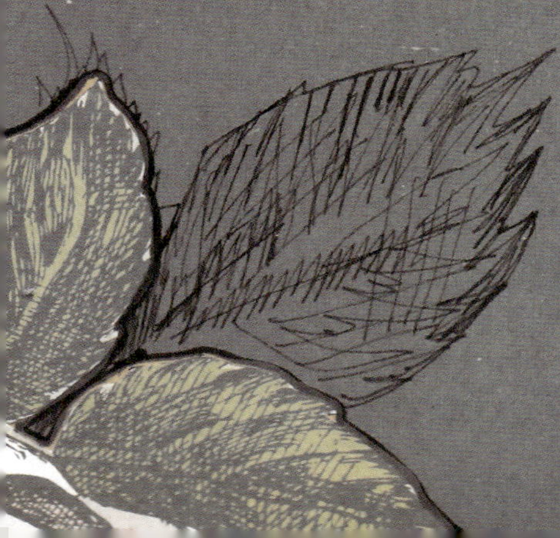

49

A Letter to Grief

when?

PAUSE FOR THOUGHT

WRITE

Analyse

STAGE 3

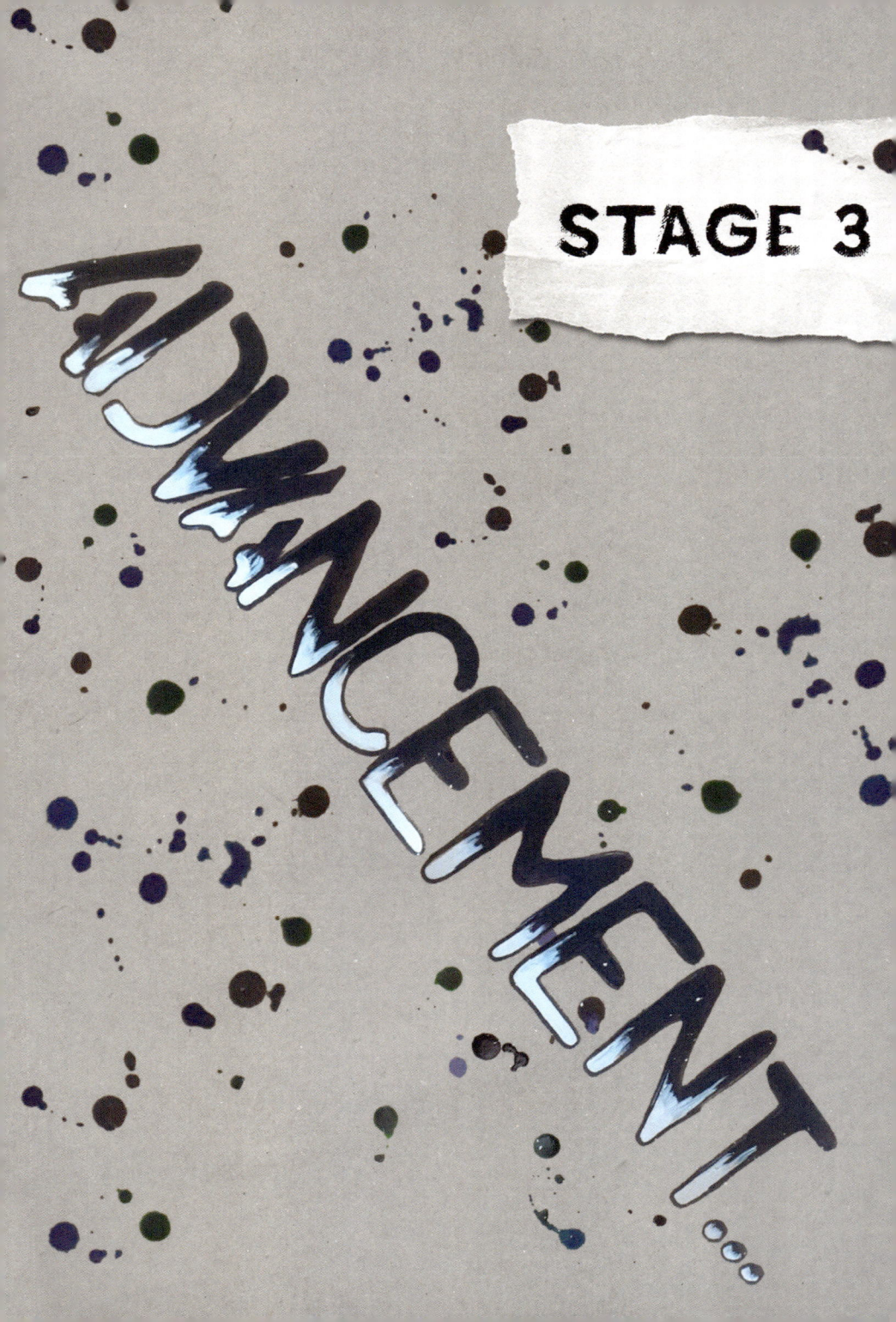

ADVANCEMENT

DECONSTRUCTION

RECONSTRUCTION

Life is constantly changing, so you are making adjustments all the time. However, getting used to someone or something familiar suddenly not being there can be extremely challenging. It may help if you think about significant changes you have already been through - how they affected you and what you did to work through them. Some changes are beneficial, while others are difficult to understand. Always keep in mind that change and how you approach it makes you who you are - it helps you grow. Losing someone or something you love is painful, so exploring these complicated feelings is important - it offers insight into what is happening. Experiencing these sensations for yourself reveals how much that person, absence or loss means to you. We form attachments to people, memories and objects as it gives us a sense of belonging and of being valued and loved. It is sometimes difficult to make sense of attachment, but these responses are natural - they are what make you human. Finding ways in which to cope will increase your resilience and help manage other changes in the future. Grief is a difficult journey. It can be a fluid process, so remember to be gentle with yourself every day. In time, the anguish will diminish, so patience and care in these early stages are very important. As you reconstruct, you will develop ways to ensure that you look after yourself.

VISUAL PRIVATE MEMOIR... Using words, images and colour in the following pages, explore how fragmented you feel and the various ways you might RECONSTRUCT and become whole again

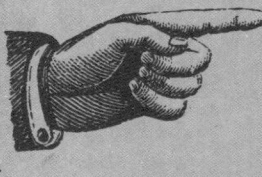

55

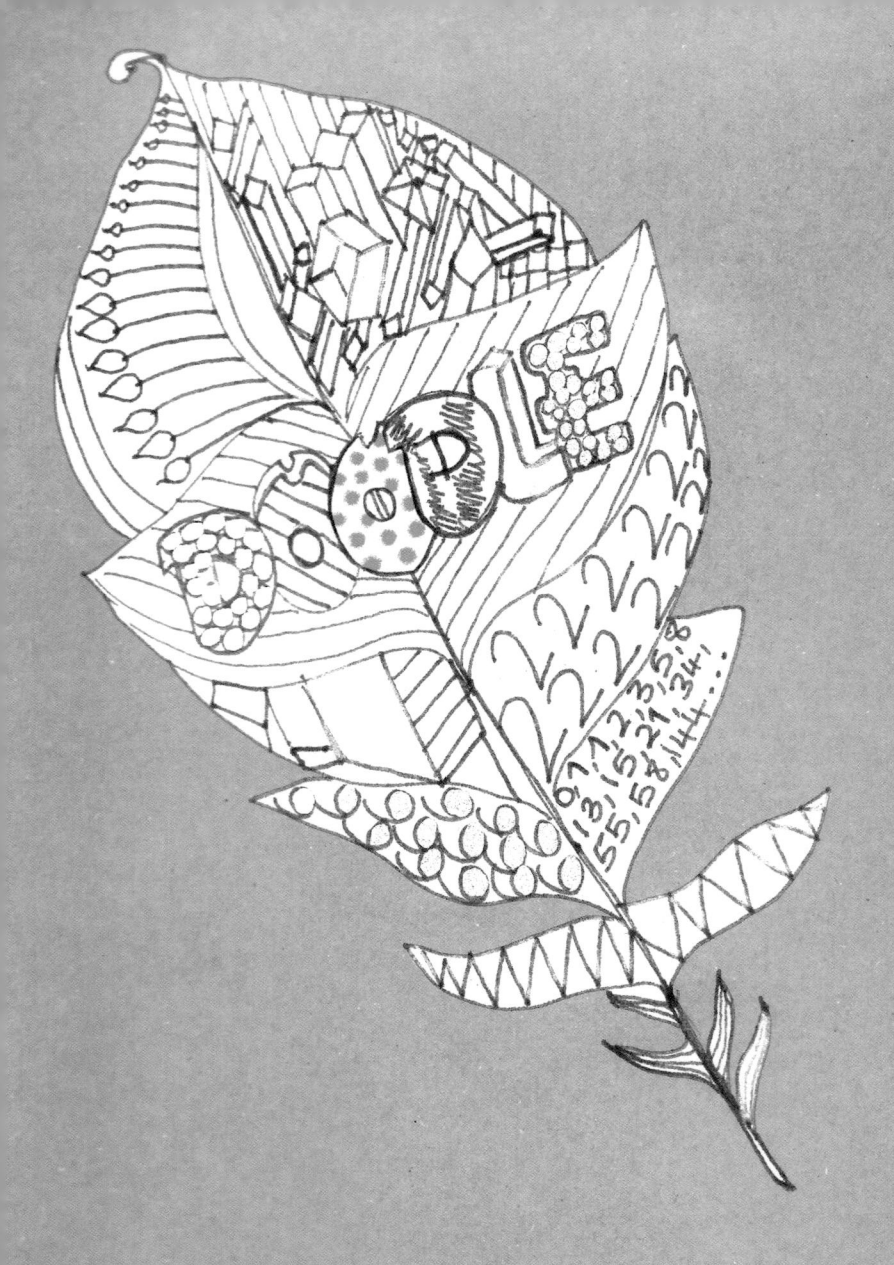

PAUSE FOR THOUGHT

reflect

DRAW

better than
than
yesterday

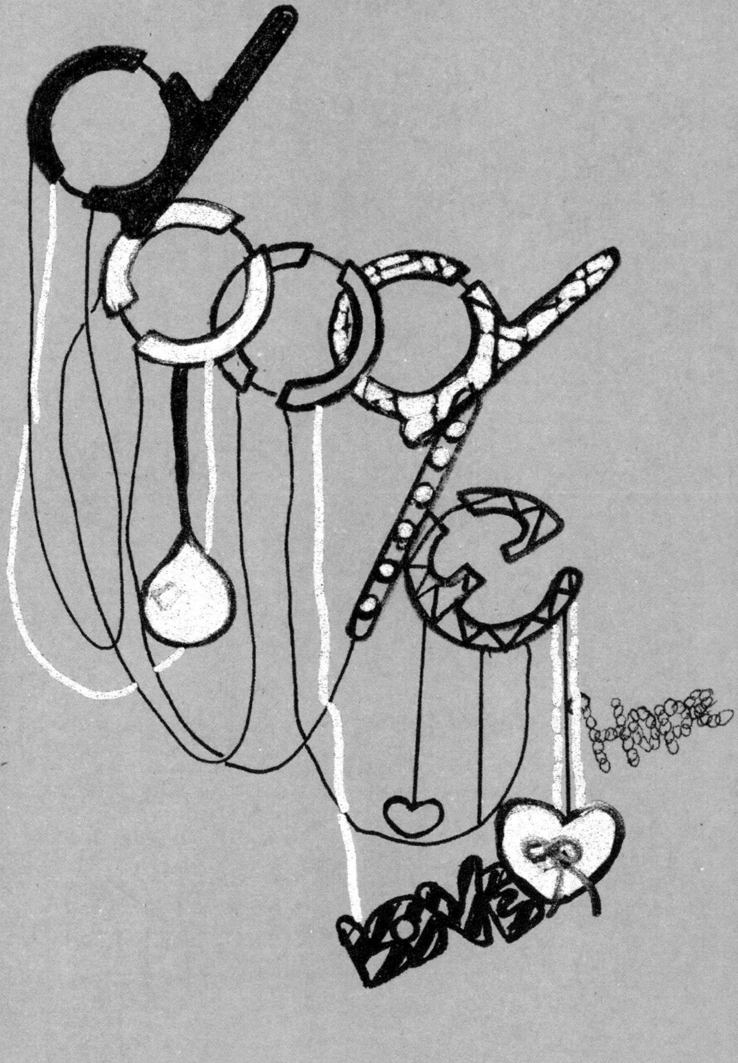

Guilt
regression
isolation
expression
focus

PAUSE FOR THOUGHT

WRITE

ANALYSE

Networks can provide

My Family

62

ORKS

invaluable support

My Friends

63

OTHER STAGES

- Avoidance
- Reflection
- Guilt
- Bargaining / Blame
- Loneliness / Despair

PAUSE FOR THOUGHT

REFLECT

LOSS IS THE WORST THING.

To bring 'em back you'd do anything.
    First week you're in denial, so you give them a ring.
The loss is so close the feeling really stings.
    All you pray for is a glimmer of hope,
And that somehow, you'll find a way to cope.
    Swimming in emotions and waves crashing down,
'*overwhelmed*' seems the only way now.
    First four months you're on a downward slope...
Depression, isolation and sadness, there's no hope!
    But trust me, good times will start to show
which is when you will slowly begin to know.
    Take it from me, it'll be a better place
and that smile will return to your face.
    A land full of beauty, a hand full of grace,
Soft earth or cremation a peaceful resting place.
    Knowing that they could never be replaced.
Holding those memories of one so clear;
    You'll recapture the essence of the places so dear.
Photos, conversations and a hand written note
    Are your way to healing and a life full of hope.
Your journal proclaims all the love you invest,
    in that something or someone that's gone to rest.

Author K.B. Whelan

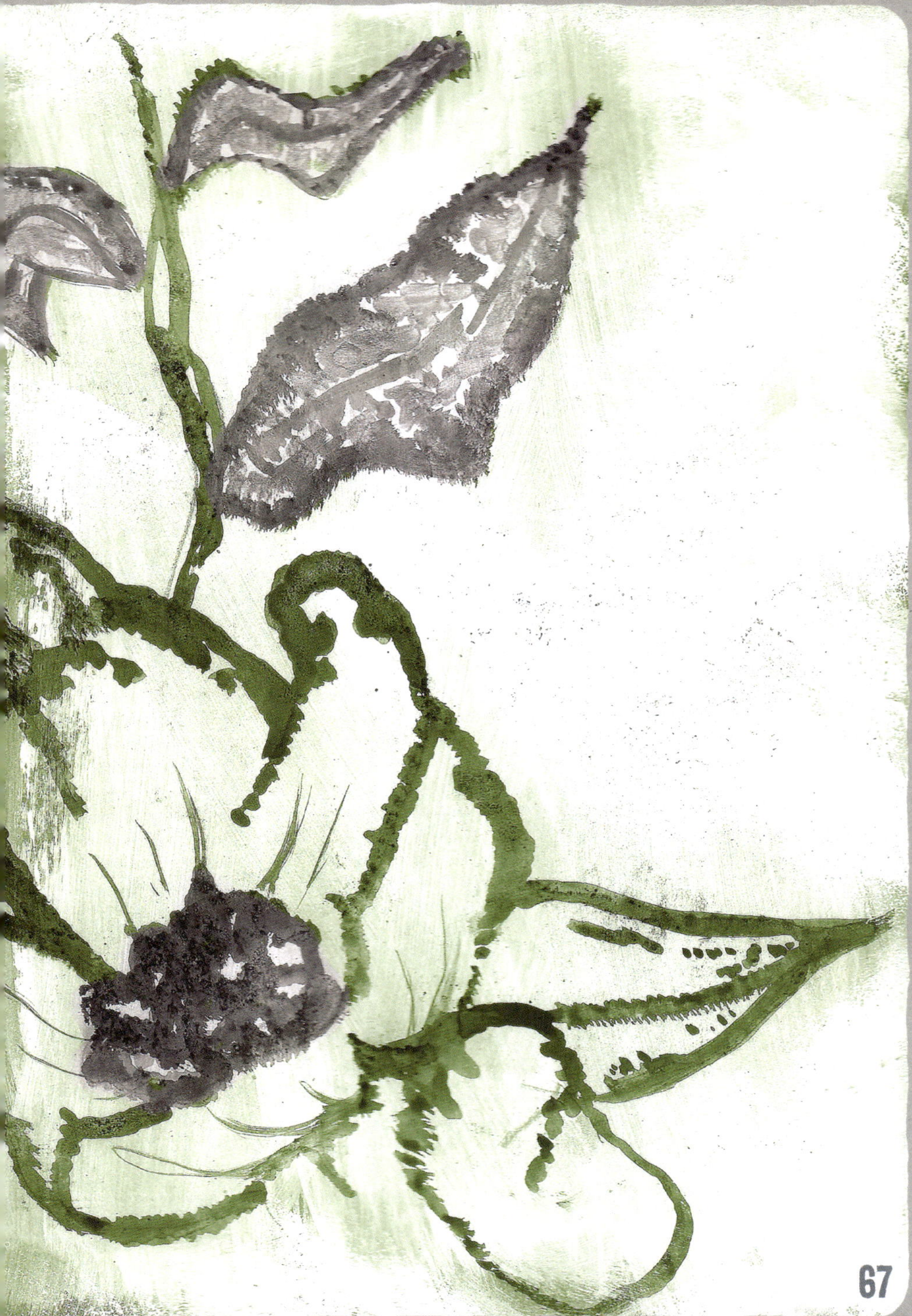

68

We can be going along feeling life is okay - then, out of nowhere grief hits us with the full force of a crashing wave. With each trigger, the force returns and strengthens without us being able to interpret those feelings.

This is normal and all part of your healing process.

It gets easier with time.

Each person's journey is unique.

COPING S

MUSIC

FRIENDS

FILM

RATEGIES

VULNERABLE

NATURE

HOBBIES

TRAVEL

Don't Let Your Life Float away

DRAW PAUSE FOR THOUGHT write

PAUSE FOR THOUGHT

REFLECT

WRITE

REVELATION

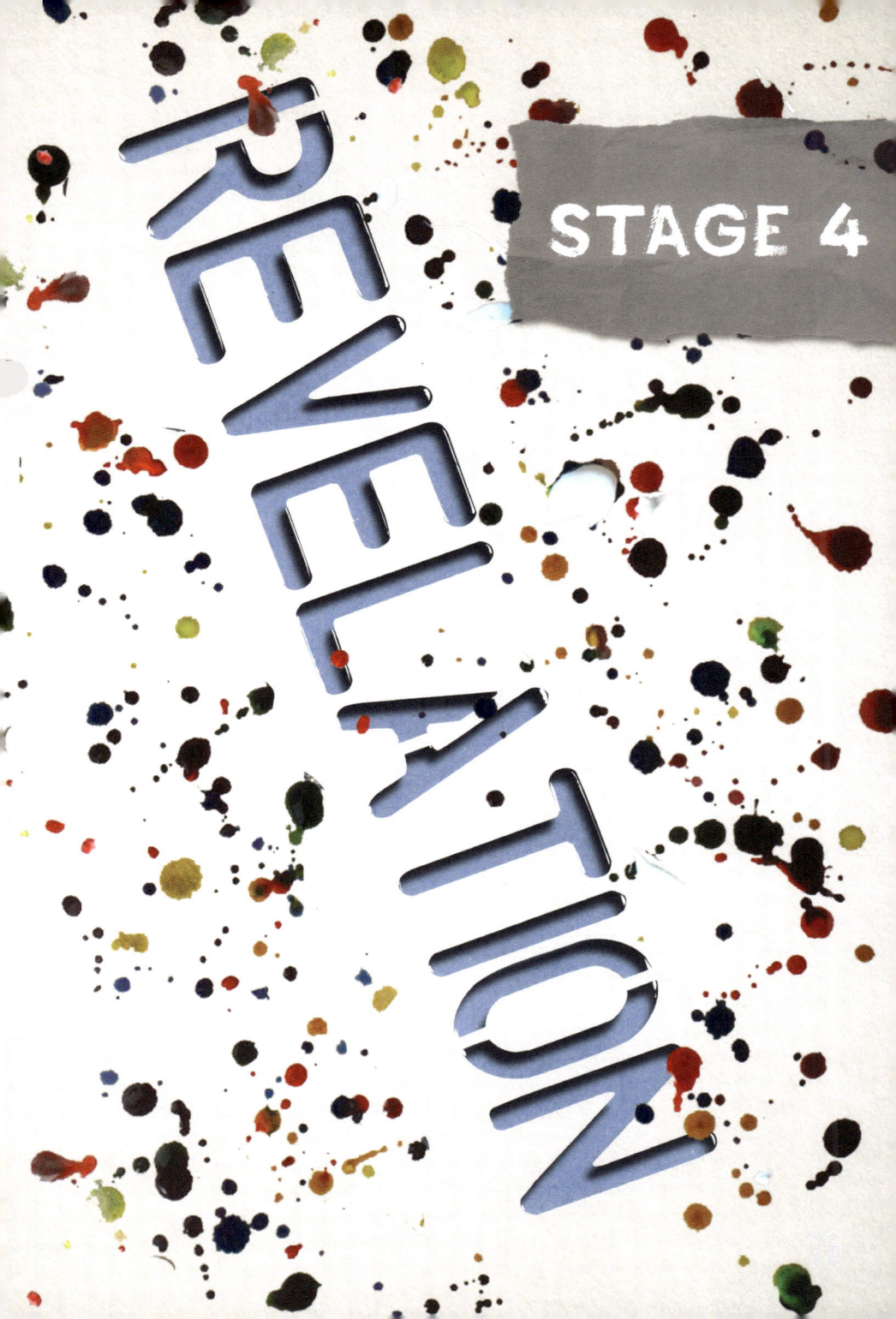

STAGE 4

GRIEF...

1. Why am I grieving?

2. The hardest time of my day is?

3. I miss ...

4. My fondest memory is ...

5. My support system includes ...

6. I wish my friends would say ...

7. The season which holds the best memories is ...

8. When I am alone, I find myself doing this ...

9. The things which would help me right now are ...

10. Who can I talk to?

11. What does coping with these changes feel like?

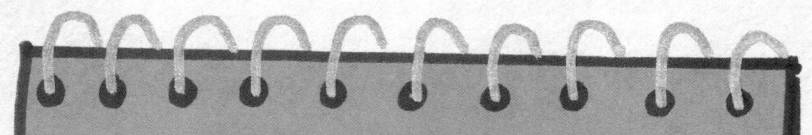

Existential Quandary

Some questions don't behave and refuse to have answers!

Make a list of your own that fall into this category.

PS: These may change over time ...

MEMORIES

PHOTOS

LOST

FOUND

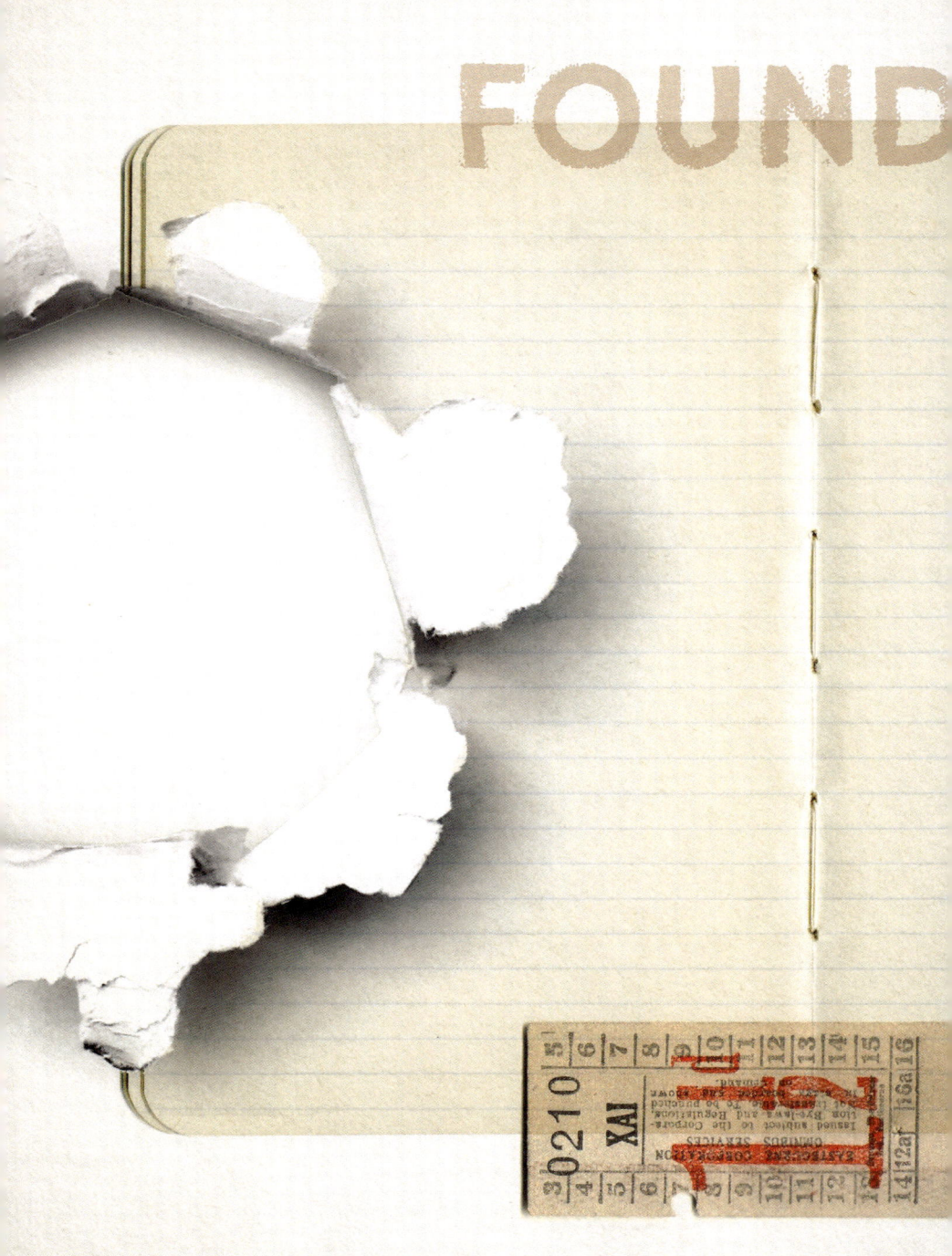

USEFUL C

> Dependent upon how you arrived to experience this grief episode, there are other agencies and charities able to help young people and maybe reaching out to them might be your next stage of your journey; self-referrals are always welcomed.

Child Bereavement UK 0800 028 8840
National organisation supporting families and training professionals in a wide range of child bereavements. **CHILDBEREAVEMENTUK.ORG**

Cruse 0808 808 1677
Cruse Bereavement Care is the leading national charity for bereaved people in England, Wales and Northern Ireland. **CRUSE.ORG.UK**

Childline 0800 1111
Help and advice through online counselling, email or message boards. **CHILDLINE.ORG.UK**

The National Bereavement Service 0800 024 6121
The NBS works alongside industry-leading professionals to offer practical and emotional support when a person dies. **BETTERHELP.COM**

British Association for Counselling & Psychotherapy 01455 883300
Offers a range of qualified therapists which charge for their service. **BACP.CO.UK**

National Counseling Society 01903 200666
The NCS is a membership body for professional counsellors, psychotherapists and psychologists. **NATIONALCOUNSELLINGSOCIETY.ORG**

Young Minds 0808 802 5544
Advice about mental health and well-being. **YOUNGMINDS.ORG.UK**

Pete's Dragons Charity 01395 277780
Bereavement support after suicide. **PETESDRAGONS.ORG.UK**

Papyrus UK 0800 068 4141
Helping children and young people under the age of 35 who are experiencing thoughts of suicide. **PAPYRUS-UK.ORG**

Rip Rap ON-SITE CONTACT FORM
This site is developed especially for teenagers who have a parent with cancer. **RIPRAP.ORG.UK**

Bereavement Advice Center 0800 634 9494
Information and advice on practical concerns after death.
BEREAVEMENTADVICE.ORG

National Self-Harm Network
The NSHN support individuals who self harm to reduce emotional distress and improve their quality of life. **NSHN.CO.UK**

Wiltshire Treehouse 01793 987 105
Local to Swindon and Wiltshire and offers bereavement support to young people and their families. **TREEHOUSEWILTSHIRE.ORG.UK**

Cruse 0808 808 1677
Free support to all bereaved people - information, counselling support and training services. **CRUSE.ORG.UK**

Dying Matters 0800 021 4466
A coalition of individual and organisations across England and Wales, which aims to help people talk openly about dying, death and bereavement and to make plans for the end of life. **DYINGMATTERS.ORG**

Maggie's Centres 0300 123 1801
Centres for anyone affected by cancer - practical, emotional and psychological support. **MAGGIES.ORG**

Samaritans 116 123 (freephone)
A confidential emotional support service for anyone in the UK and Ireland. The telephone line is open 24 hours and drop-in service. **SAMARITANS.ORG**

See Saw 01865 744768
Grief support for children and young people in Oxfordshire.
SEESAW.ORG.UK

Survivors of Bereavement by Suicide 0300 111 5065
Exists to meet the needs and break the isolation of those bereaved by the suicide of a close relative or friend. **UKSOBS.ORG**

The Compassionate Friends Local Group 0345 123 2304
Charity of bereaved parents, siblings and grandparents supporting others who have been similarly bereaved. **TCF.ORG.UK**

Winston's Wish 0808 802 0021
National childhood bereavement organisation supporting children and families facing any kind of death. **WINSTONSWISH.ORG.UK**

NHS Bereavement Helpline 0800 260 0400
Staffed by trained nurses highly skilled and experienced in working with bereaved families. 8am to 8pm every day.

Grief Encounter 0808 802 0111
Personal support and resources that can help you communicate how and what you are feeling when coping with loss.
GRIEFENCOUNTER.ORG.UK

TIC+ 01594 372 777
Counselling services in Gloucestershire. **TICPLUS.ORG.UK**

Youth Health Organization International 386 1 200 95 63
A network of organisations who work on or are related to Youth Health.
YHO.NETWORK

The Good Grief Trust 0800 260 0400
All at The Good Grief Trust have lost someone they love, so they want to help you find the support you need as quickly as possible.
THEGOODGRIEFTRUST.ORG

Kooth 0203 984 9337
Using technology to create new ways for people everywhere to access the very best mental health support and treatment. **XENZONE.COM**

Slow Group 0753 242 3674
Support for Bereaved Parents and Siblings in London.
SLOWGROUP.CO.UK

Love respect ON-SITE CONTACT FORM
national charity working to end domestic abuse against women and children. **LOVERESPECT.CO.UK**

We Are Beyond ON-SITE CONTACT FORM
Amental health charity supporting young people.
WEAREBEYOND.ORG.UK

Hub of Hope Charity ON-SITE CONTACT FORM
Offers an array of services local to the inquiries postcode.
HUBOFHOPE.CO.UK

Papyrus UK 0800 068 4141
Helping children and young people under the age of 35 who are experiencing thoughts of suicide. **PAPYRUS-UK.ORG**

Queen of Retreats ON-SITE CONTACT FORM
Your most trusting source of retreating. **QUEENOFRETREATS.COM**

Anna Freud Centre for Children and Families 020 7794 2313
A children's charity dedicated to providing training and support for child mental health services. **ANNAFREUD.ORG**

APPS

Grassroots
An award-winning charity and UK leader in suicide prevention.
PREVENT-SUICIDE.ORG.UK

My Possible Self
A holistic approach to mental health. **MYPOSSIBLESELF.COM**

Mind Gym
Transforming how people think, feel and behave at work.
THEMINDGYM.COM

Headspace
Uses meditation techniques for a happier, more well-rested life.
HEADSPACE.COM

GRIEF EPISODE GUIDE FOR TEENS
Creating a Pathway to
Resilience and Recovery

By K.B. Whelan

Inukshuk PUBLISHING

PUBLISHED IN 2020 BY INUKSHUK PUBLISHING

2022 © INUKSHUK PUBLISHING

ISBN: 978-1-5272-7534-8

INFO@INUKSHUK-PUBLISING.COM

BOOK DESIGN AND FORMATTING BY HALLIDAYBOOKS.COM

THE RIGHT OF K.B. WHELAN TO BE IDENTIFIED AS THE AUTHOR AND ILLUSTRATOR OF THIS WORK HAS BEEN ASSERTED BY HER IN ACCORDANCE WITH THE COPYRIGHT DESIGNS AND PATENTS ACT.

ALL RIGHTS RESERVED. NO PART OF THIS PUBLICATION MAY BE REPRODUCED, STORED IN A RETRIEVAL SYSTEM, OR TRANSMITTED IN ANY FORM OR BY ANY MEANS, ELECTRONIC, MECHANICAL, PHOTOCOPYING, RECORDING OR OTHERWISE WITHOUT PRIOR WRITTEN PERMISSION FROM THE PUBLISHER.

ACKNOWLEDGEMENTS
- SHIETAKA KURITA, INVENTOR OF EMOJI FOR INSPIRATION
- DR. JANINA FISHER PHD. PSYCHOTHERAPIST
- STROBE & SCHUT, 1995,'DUAL PROCESS MODEL OF COPING WITH BEREAVEMENT'
- WHOLE HEARTED SCHOOL COUNSELLING, IF FEELINGS COULD TALK...
- SCRABBLE INVENTOR ALFRED MOSHER BUTTS
- KEITH HARING, FOR HIS EMOTIONAL CONTEXT OF PHYSICAL EXPRESSION
- PHIL LISTER, FOR HIS QUOTATION: 'NORMALNESS LEADS TO SADNESS'
- PLUTCHIK'S EMOTION WHEEL LITERACY TO EXTEND THE BASIC WORDS OF FEELINGS AND EMOTIONS
- POEM: 'LOSS IS THE WORST THING' BY K.B. WHELAN

SECOND EDITION PRINTED IN UK 2022
FIRST EDITION PRINTED IN UK 2020

About the author

K.B. Whelan is a qualified clinical psychotherapist graduating with a master's in counseling and psychotherapy. Living in the UK, and operating since 2016 in private practice, she specialises in trauma and grief. Combined with a degree in Fine Art from the University of Bath in 2010, she created the *Grief Episode Guide For Teens* as the first in a series of guided interactive grief journals.

K. B. Whelan
MA, BA (HONS) DFAP,
MBACP/ACCRE MNCS PG DIP.

'This very thoughtful, interactive grief journal by Kathleen B. Whelan is a valuable and helpful resource for teenagers and young adults navigating grief.

Kathleen, very helpfully begins with an introduction to the complex process and emotions of grief through Kubler-Ross's Five Stages of Grief and then invites readers to journal their emotions and feelings. Expression of these is the first stage to the healing process, helping us become aware of our emotions, process them and move forward.

Kathleen gently advises us to honour our feelings and use the journal as a way to document and acknowledge the very difficult and challenging feelings that we go through. This can be kept private or shared, depending on how we want to use the journal. It's lightweight, ideal for a handbag/backpack so that whenever those feelings and emotions surface we can use the journal to express/jot these down. In this way, it serves as a wonderful tool to support our healing journey.

What's helpful, is that Kathleen gives us the language we might be missing to understand our feelings better from feeling ambivalence, anger, discombobulation, isolation and volatility.

What struck me about the journal is the way it's designed to capture our feelings about grief, through imagery, poetry and coping strategies. I also love the colour coding to mirror the different stages of grief and emotions that people go through as we heal'.

Bijal Shah · August 2022
Book curator, bibliotherapist, freelance journalist, author and poet

GRIEF EPISODE GUIDE FOR TEENS

Creating a Pathway to Resilience and Recovery

'*Grief Episode Guide for Teens* (Inukshuk Publishing) is an interactive journal for anyone between 12 and 25 who's suffering a loss of sorts. Written by psychotherapist Kathleen Whelan, it's useful whether you've lost a person, an item, a place or part of your identity, or if you've had a missed opportunity.

I found opening the journal for the first time quite daunting. But I instantly felt reassured reading the contents and introduction.

Knowing each step of the journal from the beginning allowed me to allocate time to each stage, depending on what I felt I could manage, and I appreciated the author's note and the reminder that grieving is a long process. It was a helpful insight too to know that seeking professional help should come after six months if needed.

As a young person experiencing grief or depression for the first time, it can be difficult to know how to articulate the way you're feeling to the people around you so learning the vocabulary to express yourself, as I did from this guide, is an invaluable skill. Quotes throughout the journal resonated with me and made me feel heard and understood.

Also, as I worked through the book and gained confidence in putting my thoughts onto paper, I found it a really helpful tool to reflect on when speaking with my counsellor.

Overall, *Grief Episode Guide for Teens* has been really helpful to me in working through my own emotions. It took me some practice to effectively use the 'pause for thought pages', but once my counsellor prompted me, I found it a good self-help tool to grab as and when I was in the right frame of mind to confront my grief.'

Rosa Murphy
On behalf of Queens of Retreats, UK